This Ordinary, Extraordinary Life

Cycle B Sermons Based on the Gospel Lessons for
Pentecost through Proper 16

April Yamasaki

CSS Publishing Company, Inc.
Lima, Ohio

THIS ORDINARY, EXTRAORDINARY LIFE

FIRST EDITION
Copyright © 2023
by CSS Publishing Co., Inc.

Published by CSS Publishing Company, Inc., Lima, Ohio 45807. All rights reserved. No part of this publication may be reproduced in any manner whatsoever without the prior permission of the publisher, except in the case of brief quotations embodied in critical articles and reviews. Inquiries should be addressed to: CSS Publishing Company, Inc., Permissions Department, 5450 N. Dixie Highway, Lima, Ohio 45807.

All scripture quotations, unless otherwise indicated, are taken from the New Revised Standard Version of the Bible. Copyright 1989 by the Division of Christian Education of the National Council of the Churches of Christ in the USA, Nashville, Thomas Nelson Publishers © 1989. Used by permission. All rights reserved.

Library of Congress Cataloging-in-Publication Data:
Names: Yamasaki, April, author.
Title: This ordinary, extraordinary life : Cycle B sermons based on the Gospel lessons for the first half of the season after Pentecost / April Yamasaki.
Description: First edition. | Lima, Ohio : CSS Publishing Company, Inc., [2023]
Identifiers: LCCN 2023028375 (print) | LCCN 2023028376 (ebook) | ISBN 9780788030864 (paperback) | ISBN 9780788030871 (adobe pdf)
Subjects: LCSH: Jesus Christ--Biography--Sermons.
Classification: LCC BV4222 .Y36 2023 (print) | LCC BV4222 (ebook) | DDC 251--dc23/eng/20230821
LC record available at https://lccn.loc.gov/2023028375
LC ebook record available at https://lccn.loc.gov/2023028376

For more information about CSS Publishing Company resources, visit our website at www.csspub.com, email us at csr@csspub.com, or call (800) 241-4056.

e-book:
ISBN-13: 978-0-7880-3087-1
ISBN-10: 0-7880-3087-6

ISBN-13: 978-0-7880-3086-4
ISBN-10: 0-7880-3086-8

PRINTED IN USA

Contents

Introduction 7

Trinity Sunday .... John 3:1-17
God in Action: Essence and Event 9

Proper 4 / Ordinary Time 9 .... Mark 2:23-3:6
Jesus and the Sabbath: Law-Abiding and Life-Giving 13

Proper 5 / Ordinary Time 10 .... Mark 3:20-35
Family, Work, and Rest 17

Proper 6 / Ordinary Time 11 .... Mark 4:26-34
Parables of Unexpected Growth and Greatness 21

Proper 7 / Ordinary Time 12 .... Mark 4:35-41
Through Storm and Calm with Jesus 25

Proper 8 / Ordinary Time 13 .... Mark 5:21-43
Power and Particularity 29

Proper 9 / Ordinary Time 14 .... Mark 6:1-13
Lessons in Perseverance and Letting Go 33

Proper 10 / Ordinary Time 15 .... Mark 6:14-29
A Gruesome Death and God's Good News 37

Proper 11 / Ordinary Time 16 .... Mark 6:30-34, 53-56
Clamoring Crowd, Compassionate Shepherd 41

Proper 12 / Ordinary Time 17 .... John 6:1-21
God of the Possible and Impossible 45

Proper 13 / Ordinary Time 18 .... John 6:24-35
Food That Perishes, Food That Endures 49

Proper 14 / Ordinary Time 19 .... John 6:35, 41-51
Bread of Earth, Bread of Heaven 53

Proper 15 / Ordinary Time 20 .... John 6:51-58
Eating and Drinking by Faith 57

Proper 16 / Ordinary Time 21 .... John 6:56-69
Turning Away or Moving Forward 61

About the Author 65

*For Gary, who said,
"You should write this book."*

Introduction

This Ordinary, Extraordinary Life is all about Jesus — and it's all about you and me and the world around us.

Jesus lived an ordinary life. He had parents, brothers and sisters, and an extended family. He worked with his hands and read the scriptures. He got hungry, thirsty, tired, just like anyone else. He loved to spend time with people — telling stories, going to parties, blessing children and their parents, and talking about things that mattered. He loved creation — spending time outdoors, walking for miles, observing and commenting on flowers and fields of grain, on trees and birds.

Jesus lived — and continues to live! — an extraordinary life. As the divine word, he was present before creation, and through him all things were created. As the second person of the Trinity, he was God Incarnate. He gave his earthly life to preaching and teaching, to healing and doing wonders. He welcomed people from all walks of life and called them to follow him. As the Bread of Life, the Bread of Heaven, he gave his life for the world. He died in humiliation and pain on a cross — then rose again to life! He returned to heaven, and one day will come again in glory.

Today my ordinary life includes making meals, doing dishes and laundry, shopping for groceries, spending time with family and friends, reading scripture, worshiping with my church, speaking, writing, editing, gardening, going for walks outdoors, eating, staying hydrated, sleeping, driving, taking the car in for service, talking on the phone, doing email, and tending to a million other things. You may have other ordinary activities that are uniquely yours, but many of the things on my list are part of your ordinary life too.

Yet by faith in Jesus, our ordinary lives can become extraordinary. Grace breaks in to the routine of daily living. Ordinary bread becomes a sign of God's kingdom. Ordinary water becomes a sign of God's living presence among us. Miracles become possible. Love and forgiveness transform our relationships. Hope abides even in the midst of disappointment and suffering. Death gives way to eternal life.

Does all this sound too good to be true? Certainly no book of sermons can express the fullness of the ordinary, extraordinary life of Jesus. And this side of heaven, our lives may feel more ordinary than extraordinary most of the time. But this is the promise of God's kingdom — that God is at work, that what starts small will grow, that with faith the ordinary can be extraordinary.

I pray these brief sermons and prayers will whet your appetite for this ordinary, extraordinary life of Jesus, for this ordinary, extraordinary life offered to you and me. If you're a preacher, I pray that you'll add your own stories and rework these sermons to make them your own, to speak most effectively to your congregation. If you're reading on your own or with a small group, you may also be interested in a free study guide for *This Ordinary, Extraordinary Life* available at AprilYamasaki.com.

Thank you for reading. May God continue to bless you in ordinary and extraordinary ways.

Trinity Sunday
John 3:1-17

God in Action: Essence and Event

Although Trinity Sunday has a designated spot in the church calendar, it doesn't seem to get the same kind of attention as some of the other special days of the year. No one says, "Merry Trinity Sunday" the way they say "Merry Christmas." Or "Happy Trinity Sunday," the way they say "Happy Easter." There are no big sales in the stores for Trinity Sunday. No three-day weekend.

Perhaps that's just as well so the Trinity doesn't get bound up in the commercialism of our world. But the lack of popular attention may also indicate how much the Trinity remains shrouded in mystery.

At the end of teaching a twelve-week class on the doctrine of the Trinity, associate professor Ben Myers issued a series of sixty-six short statements on Twitter, including:

#32. The "oneness" of God is not a number. It refers to God's incomparable mystery.

#33. The "threeness" is not a number. It refers to the incomparable fullness of the life of the one God, who is God as Father, Son & Holy Spirit.

#34. So the words "one" and "three" have to be abstracted away from their ordinary numerical meaning, and from any image of three things. The doctrine is not a mathematical puzzle.

In this series of tweets, Myers' language is understandably constrained. But clearly even for a seasoned theologian, it seems easier to say what the Trinity is not, than to say what it is.

Then too Trinity Sunday is unique because it celebrates a doctrine, instead of an event. Christmas celebrates the event of Jesus' birth, Easter the event of Jesus' resurrection, Pentecost the event of the Holy Spirit giving birth to the church. These are all significant events. But the Trinity doesn't seem to be an event in the same way. The Trinity is a doctrine, an article of belief.

But is it only that?

What if we thought of the Trinity both as a doctrine and as an event? As an article of belief AND as an experience of God at work as Father, Son, and Holy Spirit? The Triune God is indeed a doctrine concerning the essence of God. What's more, the Triune God is also an event, God in action in human life.

That at least helps me understand why the story of Jesus and Nicodemus is the Gospel Lesson for this Trinity Sunday. The word Trinity doesn't appear in the designated verses from John 3. The text doesn't try to describe the Trinity as a doctrine. Instead it shows the Trinity in action. In this chapter, the Trinity is an event. For our text shows us the way that Nicodemus could experience God in his life.

On one level, the story is clear. Nicodemus is a Pharisee, a teacher and leader among his people, and he came alone one night to talk with Jesus. But their meeting was shrouded in mystery. Why did Nicodemus come to Jesus at night? And why did he come alone? Was Nicodemus afraid to be seen with Jesus? Or was it simply easier for him to talk with Jesus at night and apart from the curious eyes of others?

Their conversation seemed a mystery for another reason too, since Jesus seemed to speak mainly in riddles. He said to enter God's kingdom, you must be born again. He spoke of wind and Spirit, of earthly things and heavenly things. And Nicodemus seemed bewildered by it all. "How can someone be born when they are old?" he asked. "How can this be?"

In our text, those were the last words that Nicodemus said to Jesus: "How can this be?" And Jesus answered the question of Nicodemus with a question of his own. "You are Israel's teacher," said Jesus, "and do you not understand these things?

Other than that, we don't know how Jesus and Nicodemus ended their conversation that night. While Jesus went on to say more, Nicodemus disappears from the storyline. Did he simply leave while Jesus was still talking? We're left hanging with his question, "How can this be?"

Yet their brief encounter gives us a clear sense of all three members of the Trinity. From the outset, when Nicodemus first approached Jesus, he said, "Rabbi, we know that you are a teacher who has come from God; for no one can do these signs that you do apart from the presence of God" (John 3:2). Nicodemus addressed Jesus with respect as "rabbi," as a fellow teacher. And he also recognized God as the one who had sent Jesus. This is God the Father, the first person of the Trinity.

Throughout the gospel of John, Jesus speaks repeatedly of the Father who sent him. "Anyone who does not honor the Son does not honor the Father who sent him" (John 5:23). "I have not spoken on my own, but the Father who sent me has himself given me a commandment what to say and what to speak" (John 12:49, cf. 6:57, 8:18, 8:42, 12:49, 13:3). As in our designated verses for today, "God [that is, the first person of the Trinity] so loved the world that he gave his one and only Son" (John 3:16).

In his encounter with Nicodemus, Jesus spoke of the Spirit, the third person of the Trinity. This is the Spirit that blows where it pleases and gives new birth. This is the same Spirit that descended on Jesus at his baptism in John 1, the Spirit that Jesus says gives life (6:63), the Spirit of truth (14:17, 15:26, 16:13), the Spirit that would come from the Father in the name of Jesus (14:26, 15:26).

And of course, Nicodemus spoke directly with Jesus, the second person of the Trinity, the Son sent from the Father not to condemn the world, but to save it (3:17). As Jesus would say later of himself, "I am the gate; whoever enters through me will be saved" (10:9). "I did not come to judge the world, but to save the world" (John 12:47).

So the three persons of the Trinity are all here in our text: the Father who loved the world so much that he sent the Son, the Son who came to save, the Spirit who brings new birth. All present and working together as one — even though the word Trinity doesn't appear in this text.

It's the same way in Romans 8:12-17. The word Trinity doesn't appear, but all three are again present and at work as one. Instead of new birth, Romans 8:14 speaks of adoption. Just as the Spirit gives new birth, so the Spirit in Romans brings about our adoption as beloved children. We are then led by the Spirit as children of God. The Spirit prompts us to cry out to God as Abba Father. And because we are God's children, we are co-heirs with Christ.

Here too, the Trinity describes how we experience God in our lives — as Abba Father who hears us when we cry out, as our Savior and co-heir who suffered and died and is now in glory, as the Spirit who makes us God's adopted children and who leads us.

That's the Triune God in action — for Nicodemus long ago, for the early Christians who received the letter to the Romans, and for us today.

Did Nicodemus experience God that way on the night he came to Jesus? The invitation was there. But was Nicodemus re-born of the Spirit? Did he call out to Abba Father? Our scripture reading doesn't tell us.

Yet a few chapters later in John 7, the chief priests and the Pharisees wanted the temple guards to arrest Jesus. The guards said, we can't do that — "Never has anyone spoken like this" (John 7:46). Nicodemus who was also present said, "Our law does not judge people without first giving them a hearing to find out what they are doing, does it?" (7:56). His words weren't exactly a statement of faith, but at least Nicodemus appeared to speak in Jesus' defense.

Then later in John 19 after Jesus had died, it was Nicodemus who went with Joseph of Arimathea to ask for the body of Jesus. It was Nicodemus who brought the spices for Jesus' burial. Again, the text does not give a direct statement of Nicodemus' faith, but he obviously had the courage and the compassion to bury Jesus' body.

We don't know how the Father, Son, and Holy Spirit might have continued to work in the life of Nicodemus. Once again he disappears from the storyline, as his name doesn't appear anywhere in the Bible after the gospel of John. His story remains unfinished.

For us too, our stories are not yet finished. The Triune God is still at work in our lives and in the world around us: the Spirit still blowing where it will to bring new life, the Son still saving us, the Father still loving the world beyond all measure. That's the Triune God in action this Trinity Sunday and every day.

Creator, Redeemer, Sustainer — we cannot fully understand the mystery of the Trinity, yet we experience your presence. We see your work in the world, we see your work in and through other people, and sense it deep within our souls. We give thanks that your Spirit continues to move among us, Jesus continues to walk with us, and the Creator of all things continues to hold us close. All praise and honor to you, the Triune God in action. Amen.

Proper 4 / Ordinary Time 9
Mark 2:23-3:6

Jesus and the Sabbath: Law-Abiding and Life-Giving

Most Sunday mornings, I'm either preaching or co-hosting my church's Zoom worship or both. Before the coronavirus pandemic, we had no thought of live streaming our worship or meeting online in any way. But when pandemic restrictions prevented us from meeting in person, we started worshiping over Zoom, and have continued with hybrid worship, meeting both online and in person.

Some worship online due to chronic health conditions or mobility issues. Some log on when they're traveling so they can still be part of the congregation from afar. One Sunday, our Zoom worship included two people in Australia, one church member traveling in France, and the rest of us from our local area. Worshiping over Zoom is definitely not the same as being in person, but the technology has helped us reach beyond our physical space.

I love preaching, co-hosting worship, and fostering our online relationships, but a steady diet of that Sunday after Sunday is not exactly restful. I need to prepare ahead of time. I sign in early and am usually the last to sign off. One Sunday due to technical difficulties, I suddenly had to email everyone a new Zoom link.

So as a Sunday morning alternative, I've started observing a Sabbath Wednesday morning. With no online responsibilities, and that includes no email and no social media. No preaching commitments. No meetings. No phone calls to schedule this or that.

To some, all these "no's" might sound like a list of rules. But to me, they spell freedom. For when I say no to such things, I can instead go for a walk, meet a friend, read scripture, pray, journal, play piano, take a nap, write a letter, make a donation, plan a celebratory lunch — not all at the same time and not in any regimented way, but to rest from work and be refreshed. Each week I look forward to my Sabbath Wednesday morning.

The Sabbath was meant to be that kind of life-giving, sacred pause. It was to be a day of blessing as in Genesis 2:3: "So God blessed the seventh day and hallowed it, because on it God rested from all the work that he had done in creation." Keeping the Sabbath became part of the ten commandments not to make life more difficult, but as a sign of the freedom God had given to the people:

> Remember that you were slaves in Egypt and that the Lord your God brought you out of there with a mighty hand and an outstretched arm. Therefore the Lord your God has commanded you to observe the Sabbath day. — Deuteronomy 5:15

In the gospels, keeping the Sabbath was a way of life. The people were to stop working just as directed in the ten commandments:

> On it you shall not do any work, neither you, nor your son or daughter, nor your male or female servant, nor your animals, nor any foreigner residing in your towns. — Exodus 20:10

That meant no baking, no hammering, no sewing, no reaping, no work of any kind.

In our Gospel Lesson today, the Pharisees questioned Jesus about the behavior of his disciples who had been walking through a field and plucking grain to eat. The religious law permitted this in Deuteronomy 23:25:

> If you go into your neighbor's standing grain, you may pluck the ears with your hand, but you shall not put a sickle to your neighbor's standing grain.

So it was permitted if you were simply passing through, to pick someone else's grain by hand and eat it. But it was against the law to go in with a sickle and a big bushel basket to cart the grain away. In this way, the law respected the owner of the field and protected his harvest, while also providing for travelers and caring for the poor. So by picking grain to eat, Jesus' disciples acted well within the religious law.

The only problem was that they did this on the Sabbath. In their zeal for the law, the Pharisees saw this as a form of reaping. In their view, Jesus' disciples were breaking the law by working on the Sabbath. But Jesus defended his disciples by pointing to the story of David long ago. In 1 Samuel 21, King Saul wanted to kill David, so David was on the run for his life. He and his men were in a hurry, passing quickly through the city. They were hungry, and the only bread available was the bread set aside for the priests. It was against the religious law for anyone else to eat that bread just as it was against the religious law to reap on the Sabbath.

But David ate the bread that was reserved by law for the priests. He even gave the bread to his companions. The Pharisees could hardly argue against David, who had become a great king and a well-respected part of their own history. Even they had to admit that David had acted with good reason to provide food for himself and his men. As Jesus said, "The sabbath was made for humankind, and not humankind for the sabbath" (Mark 2:27).

Jesus' defense silenced the Pharisees — but only for a time. They continued to watch him with critical eyes. When Jesus went into the synagogue and saw a man with a withered hand, our Gospel Lesson says that the Pharisees "watched him to see whether he would cure him on the sabbath, so that they might accuse him" (Mark 3:2). They knew that Jesus had already cured a man of an unclean spirit on a Sabbath day (Mark 1:21-28). Would he cure this man too?

They didn't seem to have any doubts that Jesus would be able to heal the man's withered hand. After all, Jesus had already healed Simon's mother-in-law. Jesus had already cured a man of leprosy. Jesus had already healed a paralyzed man. But now it was the Sabbath day. Would Jesus heal the man with the withered hand — even though healing was a kind of work? Even though healing meant breaking the Sabbath? What would Jesus do?

The man with the withered hand did not call attention to himself. Unlike blind Bartimaeus in Mark 10, he did not call out, "Jesus, Son of David, have mercy on me!" He did not ask Jesus for healing.

But Jesus noticed him and called him forward. Instead of pretending he didn't see the man or healing him quietly, Jesus did not hide what he was about to do even though he knew the Pharisees were watching him. In fact, he turned to them and pointedly asked, "Is it lawful to do good or to do harm on the sabbath, to save life or to kill?" (verse 4).

When they did not answer, Jesus was both angry and sad at their stubbornness. How could such educated and devout men focus on the details of the religious law, yet miss the whole point? How could they not see the Sabbath connection between God setting the people free from slavery long ago, and God in Jesus Christ now setting this man free from his withered hand? How sad that they could not put the two together.

Then Jesus turned to the man and asked him to stretch out his hand. As soon as the man stretched it out, his hand was restored to full strength!

But instead of celebrating the miracle, the Pharisees went on with their plan to accuse Jesus. They met with the Herodians, a group that is mentioned just three times in scripture (Matthew 22:16; Mark 3:6, 12:13). According to Josephus, a first-century historian, the Herodians were supporters of Herod the Great. While the devout Pharisees did not share their political views, their mutual opposition to Jesus made them allies.

It is ironic that while Jesus did good and healed on the Sabbath day, his opponents sought to do harm and to destroy him. While Jesus sought to restore the fullness of life, his opponents plotted to kill him. Jesus' earlier question about doing good or harm on the Sabbath, saving a life or killing took on an even deeper significance because it was not only a question about the man with the withered hand. It was not only a question about what Jesus would do. It was also a question about the Pharisees. This was their Sabbath — would they use it to do good or harm, to save life or kill? Tragically, the keepers of the Sabbath took action to do harm.

In this the Pharisees stood in sharp contrast with Jesus. They sought to do harm. He sought to heal. They practiced the letter of the law. Jesus practiced the law's life-giving spirit. By claiming authority over the Sabbath, by claiming authority to do good and to save life seven days a week, by claiming authority over the religious and political realities of the day, Jesus claimed lordship over everything: "The Son of Man is Lord even of the sabbath" (Mark 2:28).

Lord of the Sabbath, you are Lord of everything, including the way we use our time. Guide us in using it wisely and well, with a healthy rhythm of worship, work, and Sabbath rest. May we do good and not harm. May we act in life-giving ways on the Sabbath and every day. Amen.

Proper 5 / Ordinary Time 10
Mark 3:20-35

Family, Work, and Rest

Last week I received this email from the pastor of another church: "You are so busy! Make sure you take some time off to relax. Please take care of yourself."

We might well understand Jesus' family thinking the same thing about Jesus. He was so busy — healing crowds of people, facing criticism from the religious leaders, calling and appointing his disciples, going to the synagogue, and even curing a man's withered hand on the Sabbath. Even now that he was "home" — perhaps at the home of Simon and Andrew in Capernaum (Mark 1:29) — Jesus had no time to relax. He hardly had time to eat!

So Jesus' family tried to "restrain" him. The word used here means to take charge or to arrest someone. Like Herod's men who arrested John the Baptist (Mark 6:17) or the crowd who came to arrest Jesus in the garden of Gethsemane (Mark 14:46). In our Gospel Lesson, Jesus' family wanted to "arrest" him, that is to stop him. To them, Jesus seemed so "out of his mind," so beside himself, that they were concerned for his physical and mental well-being. They wanted to take charge of whatever would happen next. Perhaps they meant to take him to their family home in Nazareth, away from the crowds and their endless demands, where he could have a meal in peace and rest.

The scribes from Jerusalem went even further. In their view, Jesus was more than simply exhausted and overworked. They said that he cast out demons by Beelzebul, the ruler of the demons. It wasn't the only time that Jesus was accused of being possessed by a demon. Others said the same thing after hearing Jesus talk about being both the gate for the sheep and the good shepherd. Many said, "He has a demon and is out of his mind. Why listen to him?" (John 10:20).

But Jesus pointed out the flaw in the reasoning of the scribes. How could he possibly cast out demons by the ruler of the demons? That would be the end of Satan's power, which the scribes were not prepared to admit. To this, Jesus added a warning that "whoever blasphemes against the Holy Spirit can never have forgiveness" (Mark 3:29). Jesus didn't directly accuse the scribes of blasphemy, but the implication was clear. By refusing to recognize God's Spirit at work in Jesus, by attributing his work instead to the ruler of the demons, they committed a serious offense against the Spirit of God. By doing so, they set themselves outside of the forgiveness that God's Spirit offered them. For how could they receive forgiveness by the Spirit of God while at the same time denying the work of the Spirit?

The scribes had no answer for Jesus, and Jesus did not belabor the point. His family was still waiting for him. Not only whatever family members happened to be in Capernaum, but his mother and brothers who had come from Nazareth and sent him a message that they were waiting for him outside. They couldn't get into the house because of the crowd, and besides, they wanted him to come out to a quieter place.

But instead of going outside to meet them, Jesus said, "Who are my mother and my brothers?" Then he looked at those sitting around him and said, "Here are my mother and my brothers! Whoever does the will of God is my brother and sister and mother" (Mark 3:35).

With these words, Jesus broadened the definition of family to include anyone who does the will of God. For Jesus, family is not about sharing the same DNA or sharing the same experience of growing up in the same household. Instead, family is defined by a shared commitment and a shared way of life in the household of God.

Of course we know that Jesus was part of a human family. Countless Christmas cards focus on the baby Jesus with his mother, Mary, and with Joseph as the father who raised him as his own. The gospel of Matthew mentions Jesus' sisters, and even lists the names of his brothers, James Joseph, Simon, and Judas (Matthew 13:55). The gospel of Luke describes John the Baptist and his parents, Zechariah and Elizabeth, who is identified as a relative of Mary (Luke 1:36). So in addition to Mary and Joseph, Jesus' family included his sisters and brothers, plus an extended family of other relatives.

Jesus would have been very familiar with the religious law to "honor your father and mother." He even included it in his own teaching, for when a man came to Jesus and asked, "What must I do to inherit eternal life?" Jesus referred him to the ten commandments and made a point of listing the command to honor one's parents (Luke 18:18-25).

He had a close and caring relationship with his mother, Mary. At her prompting, he performed his first public miracle at the wedding of Cana. In the last hours of his life on the cross, he honored his mother by ensuring that she would be cared for after his death. His father,

Joseph, had likely already passed on by that time, and as the oldest son, he took responsibility for his mother's care. So in addition to the care provided by his brothers and sisters and other relatives, Jesus appointed one of his disciples to care for her as his own mother (John 19:26-27).

Yet while Jesus honored his mother, our Gospel Lesson makes clear that Mary and the rest of his family didn't fully understand his ministry. That's why they sought to stop him — not only because they cared for his health, but because they didn't understand the force and importance of his mission. They didn't understand that God had sent him to give himself to preaching, teaching, and healing, and that one day he would give his life on the cross.

Jesus clearly worked hard at giving himself to ministry. But he also took time to rest and taught his disciples to do the same. After a long day with the crowds, Jesus slept in the stern of the boat while his disciples set sail for the other side of the lake. While traveling through Samaria, Jesus sat at a well to rest while his disciples went into town to get some food. He took time by himself away from the crowds to rest and be refreshed by God. When his disciples returned from several days of teaching and healing, he urged them to join him in a quiet place where they could get something to eat, to rest and recharge.

Jesus' family didn't need to worry about him. The rhythm of work and rest embedded in creation and embedded in the Sabbath was Jesus' own rhythm. And it's a rhythm for all of us. Not only for Jesus and his disciples long ago, not only for pastors today, but for all who follow Jesus.

In Jesus' day, people and their work were more tied to the rhythms of the seasons, to the light of day and the darkness at night. Today electric lights and electronic devices mean we can work around the clock. We can work across time zones. We can work with people around the world. We have the ability to work all of the time — but that doesn't mean it's healthy or necessary.

So yes, no matter how busy you like to be, or how busy you think you have to be, take time to relax and take care of yourself. You are not God. You are human. Accept your limitations. Trust in God. Instead of trying to control your day and your schedule, honor Jesus as the Lord of the Sabbath and the Lord of all of our days.

Instead of trying to take charge of him, Jesus' family needed to let him take charge of their lives. Instead of standing outside of his teaching, they needed to come in and learn from him like those who were gathered around him in our Gospel Lesson.

For us too, let us attend to Jesus' example and teaching. May we accept his gracious invitation to rest and learn from him:

> Come to me, all you that are weary and are carrying heavy burdens, and I will give you rest. Take my yoke upon you, and learn from me; for I am gentle and humble in heart, and you will find rest for your souls. For my yoke is easy, and my burden is light. — Matthew 11:28-30

Dear Jesus, what an honor to be included in your family, to know your welcome and forgiveness. Yet your words continue to challenge us: "Whoever does the will of God is my brother and sister and mother." When we falter and fail, restore us. When we need your guidance, lead us. Teach us God's will and way, and grant us the grace to follow. Amen.

Proper 6 / Ordinary Time 11
Mark 4:26-34

Parables of Unexpected Growth and Greatness

Jesus loved to tell stories, and through his eyes, it seemed as if everyone and everything had a story to tell. A father watching and waiting for his estranged son, and finally welcoming him home. A shepherd going after a missing sheep. A woman searching for her lost coin. A lamp on a stand. Bread rising in a bowl. In Jesus' teaching, all these ordinary objects and everyday situations spoke powerfully about God's extraordinary kingdom.

So too in our Gospel Lesson for today. Jesus tells the parable of the growing seed and the parable of the mustard seed to teach the people about the kingdom of God. Our text records them without commentary, noting only that Jesus spoke in parables to those who came to listen, "but he explained everything in private to his disciples."

In other words, these parables were not only for Jesus' inner circle, not only for those who had chosen to follow him, who had already come to know him and to trust him. Like the other parables told by Jesus, these two parables were for the crowds — for those who came to hear Jesus only because their friends were there, for those drawn by his teaching yet not quite ready to accept it, for those who came to criticize, for those who were simply curious.

These two parables were for everyone in the crowd around Jesus, and they are also for every one of us today — whether we think of ourselves as long-time followers of Jesus, whether we're only here because our friends are here, whether we're feeling critical or bored or curious. The kingdom of God that Jesus spoke of is for all of us, and all of us matter.

At the same time, as parables, these two stories don't tell us everything that we might want to know about God's kingdom. Instead of providing a complete description, Jesus offers just a glimpse. In other places, he would say that God's kingdom is like yeast added to flour (Luke:13:20-21), or like a man who invited many guests to a great banquet (Luke 14:15-24). Or the kingdom of heaven is like treasure hidden in a field (Matthew 13:44), or like a net with all kinds of fish (Matthew

13:47-48). In the gospel of Mark, these two parables offer another part of the picture.

In the first parable, an unidentified "someone" scattered some seed. Whether from inexperience, ignorance, or some other reason, the one who scattered the seed apparently did nothing more. He didn't weed his field. He didn't water the maturing plants. He didn't protect his crop from birds. Yet the seed would sprout and grow while the man slept and went about his day. The earth gave rise to the stalk and the full head of grain, until the harvest was ready, and only then did the "someone" get to work and reap the harvest.

None of that happened immediately. It took days and nights for the seed to grow until harvest. And the one who scattered the seed didn't know how it happened. It was as if the seed nurtured by the earth grew by itself. It's growth remained a mystery.

The seed of the kingdom growing secretly was amply demonstrated in the life and ministry of Jesus. A touch of his hand, and a blind man received his sight. A word from Jesus, and sins were forgiven, a crippled man able to get up and walk. How did that happen? It must have seemed a mystery, for the crowds couldn't see the power go out from Jesus. Yet clearly God was at work — healing the sick and making people whole again, restoring people to their families and to their community.

So it is with the kingdom of God today. While we may scatter the seeds of good news, while we may sow good deeds in our community and world, the growth of God's kingdom remains a mystery. We don't know how the seeds will grow. We don't know how long it will be before the harvest. All that is a mystery to us. But God's unseen power is at work. God works in unseen, unexpected ways.

In Jesus' second parable, a tiny mustard seed grows into a large shrub. Jesus used exaggerated language to make his point, calling the mustard seed "the smallest of all the seeds on earth," and the mature plant "the greatest of all shrubs." In fact, some seeds are even smaller than the lowly mustard seed, and some shrubs larger than the mature plant. But Jesus' point is clear: just as a tiny seed can grow into a large bush, the kingdom of God starts small and becomes great.

That too was amply demonstrated in the life and ministry of Jesus. His earthly life began in a small way with his birth as an infant. Even as a grown man, he was not considered particularly great in the eyes of the world. He was just one voice preaching and teaching to the crowds. He died a humiliating and painful death on a cross. The kingdom of God seemed very small indeed.

Yet from that humble beginning came a tremendous result. Jesus rose from the dead! His disciples were transformed from hiding in fear behind locked doors to spreading the good news to all who would listen. Through faith in him, we have forgiveness from sin and the power to live a new and eternal life. We have hope for the future. Jesus' lone voice long ago has echoed through the centuries, and today people all over the world sing his praises. What began so small, turned out to be so significant. That's God's kingdom.

What's more, Jesus' choice of the mustard seed tells us that the kingdom of God won't look the way we might expect. In his day, the people had great expectations of the coming kingdom and what it would do for them. They believed God's kingdom would be a great and mighty kingdom, that it would come in great and sudden power, to put all of their enemies under their feet, and deliver them from oppression. If the crowds were to choose a symbol for this mighty kingdom, it wouldn't have been the small mustard seed and the common mustard shrub. More likely, they would have chosen a stately tree, perhaps one of the great cedars of Lebanon. After all, in the Old Testament tradition, both the psalms and the prophets describe Israel as a cedar of Lebanon, as a towering, mighty tree.

In contrast, Jesus' unexpected choice of the lowly mustard plant must have caught the attention of his listeners. It made them listen, and vividly demonstrated that God's kingdom would look different than anyone might have expected.

That was certainly true in Jesus' own life and ministry. People might have expected their king to be born in a castle, but Jesus was born in humble circumstances. When he entered Jerusalem for the last time, people might have expected their king to come in triumph mounted on a horse, but he entered the city riding on a donkey. Instead of a great display of power, Jesus died on a cross. Humanly speaking, none of those things looked like the kingdom of God. But that's exactly what God's kingdom is like — it starts small and ends big, it doesn't look the way we expect, and grows in a mysterious, unseen way.

Today, some people might look for God's kingdom to come in a grand, dramatic style. They might look for it in mega-churches and in signs and wonders. They might look for it in overseas mission or inner-city service. And they might well find God's kingdom in such places. But these two parables of Jesus suggest that real kingdom-power is also found in very ordinary places among very ordinary people — like someone scattering seed, and a small seed growing into a sizeable bush.

What small seeds have you scattered? Where are you hoping for growth where nothing seems to be happening? How is the kingdom of God different from your expectations?

By God's grace, the things that may look so small and insignificant have a hidden power that can transform you and me and the world around us. Just as a tiny mustard seed grows into a large shrub, the small and apparently insignificant things of God's kingdom can have amazing, unexpected, and extraordinary results.

When nothing seems to be happening, God is at work — working beneath the surface of outward appearances that we can see with our own eyes. So don't discount the small things of life — the warm greeting, the simple act of hospitality, teaching a child to pray, a walk with a neighbor, reaching out to a stranger, donating a bag of groceries to the food bank, writing a letter, praying for peace. Remember, the kingdom of God starts small, then grows and grows. The kingdom of God will look different than we might expect.

So whatever the coming week holds for you — baking bread, looking for something you've lost, watching and waiting for a loved one, praying for the needs of the world — be encouraged and wait for these small things to grow. Watch for the unexpected growth and greatness of the kingdom of God.

Creator God of all things ordinary and extraordinary, open our eyes to the in-breaking of your kingdom. When we get tired of watching and waiting for you, when we become impatient, encourage our hearts and lift our spirits. Surprise us with the unexpected growth of small things, with the unexpected glimpse of your greatness in the midst of daily life. Amen.

Proper 7 / Ordinary Time 12
Mark 4:35-41

Through Storm and Calm with Jesus

Today's lesson from the gospel of Mark tells a vivid story about a furious storm that Jesus made completely calm. But when Jesus stilled the winds, the disciples became terrified at the display of his power. The New Revised Version and most other English versions of the Bible use a variety of different words to describe what happened.

But the wording of the original Greek is actually more focused. Instead of a variety of different words, there's one word that's repeated several times: the Greek word "mega" which means "great." We know that a megaphone can amplify the sound of a voice and make it sound greater than it would be otherwise. A megaburger is the one with three hamburger patties, Swiss cheese, mushrooms, bacon, and anything else you can think of, that makes it so much more than just another burger.

In our Gospel Lesson, the "great windstorm" was not just any storm — the Greek text calls it a "mega" storm. Then when Jesus rebuked the wind and the waves, and there was calm, the Greek text describes it as "mega" calm. At the end of the story, the disciples were not only afraid — they were "mega" afraid. That word "mega" is repeated again and again, so this is a story about a great storm, a great calm, and a great fear.

This mega story begins and ends with Jesus. Jesus had been teaching the disciples and crowds of people all day. He had told story after story about the sower who went out to sow some seed, about a lamp on a stand, about faith like a mustard seed planted in the ground. There were so many people listening to Jesus that at one point, Jesus got into a boat and sat out in the lake speaking to the people who were lined up along the shore at the water's edge.

It was a very long day of ministry for Jesus. So when evening finally came, Jesus and his disciples pulled out into the lake and left the crowds behind. Or, at least they tried to. But some of the people followed by getting into their own boats and also pulling out into the lake.

On one side of the water was an open plain that was known for its fertile soil — that was farm country, and quite likely why Jesus' teaching so often included farmers sowing seed and growing plants. But mountains surrounded the rest of the lake. That combination of the plain on one side and mountain on the other meant that storms could come up very quickly and be as severe as storms on the open sea. That's what happened in our story. Without warning, a furious wind came up with waves so tall that they broke over the boat.

Now Jesus was so tired after his long day of teaching that he had fallen asleep in the stern of the boat. The howling wind didn't wake him. The waves crashing over the side of the boat didn't disturb him.

At the first sign of bad weather, the disciples might have thought, let's just let Jesus sleep. Many of them were experienced fishermen who had fished that same lake for years. They'd handled bad weather many times before. They knew what to do. But this time nothing they did seemed to make any difference. For all of their skill and experience, their boat remained in grave danger.

So the disciples woke Jesus up saying, "Teacher, do you not care if we are perishing?" In our English translation, this is a desperate question. But the original Greek is not as clear. It might have been a question — "Teacher, don't you care that we are perishing?" Or it may have been a statement, an accusation: "Teacher, you don't care that we are perishing."

But Jesus did care. Awakened by the disciples, Jesus got up and said to the waves, "Peace! Be still!" And just as quickly as the storm had arisen — in fact, even more quickly — the storm disappeared. The winds became quiet. The waves no longer towered over the boat and tossed it around. Everything became completely calm. Jesus had saved the disciples from the mega storm by giving them a mega calm.

You'd think the disciples would have been mega relieved, that they would have given thanks and praise to God. But that's not what happened. Instead, after the great storm and after the great calm, the disciples were mega afraid. "Who then is this?" they asked each other. How could it be that the Jesus they knew as teacher, the Jesus who was so tired that he slept through the storm, could command the wind and the waves to be still?

After all, in the Hebrew scriptures, only God could rule the sea. That was part of their history when God led the Hebrew people out of Egypt, God parted the waters of the Red Sea so the people could walk on dry ground. Psalm 89:8-9 says, "O Lord God of hosts, who is as mighty as you, O Lord? Your faithfulness surrounds you. You rule the raging of the sea; when its waves rise, you still them." That's exactly what Jesus did. So could he truly be the Lord of all creation? For the disciples, that thought was terrifying!

In response to their fear, Jesus asked them, "Why are you afraid? Have you still no faith?" With these words, Jesus challenged his disciples to move beyond their fear to put their faith in him.

They had seen with their own eyes how Jesus had used his power to teach, to heal, and now to still the storm. Jesus had used his power not to destroy them but to save them. They could have faith in God, they could trust God, because they could trust Jesus.

The Almighty One was not asleep and indifferent to their distress. The God of all creation was not unfeeling or uncaring. The Lord of all was not a God who ruled by remote control sending a storm here and a storm there to make life difficult. No — the Almighty God of Creation and Lord of All was right there with them in the person of Jesus.

Today, God in Jesus Christ is also with us, in whatever storms, in whatever calm we face in life. Psalm 9 gives us a glimpse of the storm and calm of the psalmist's life, for it speaks of times of trouble and times of praise, times of need and affliction, and times of trust in God. The psalmist knew both storm and calm in his life, and verse 10 offers this assurance of God's faithfulness through it all: "for you, O Lord, have not forsaken those who seek you."

2 Corinthians 6:1-10 gives us a glimpse of the storm and calm of the apostle's life. He writes of troubles, hardships and distress, beatings, imprisonments and riots, hard work, sleepless nights and hunger. We might think of all of those as a kind of storm. But he also lists purity, understanding, patience and kindness; being in the Holy Spirit and in sincere love — what we might think of as times of calm. And this letter too includes an assurance of God's faithfulness, as the apostle says: "see, now is the day of salvation!" (verse 2).

I suppose that each of us could look at our lives and identify times of calm and storm — in our personal lives, as households and families, as a church, as a society and country, as a global community. God has also been faithful to us, just like Jesus in the boat with his disciples, just like the Lord as a stronghold for the psalmist, just as God continued to bestow favor on the apostle. So whatever storm or calm we face today and in the future, let us respond with faith instead of fear.

Let us be like those in Psalm 107 who went out in ships and encountered a fierce storm. Psalm 107:26 says, "They mounted up to heaven, they went down to the depths; their courage melted away in their calamity" as their ships were tossed on the waves. As their ships kept moving up and down and from side to side, "they reeled and staggered like drunkards" (verse 27). They could hardly stay on their feet!

Then they cried to the Lord in their trouble, and he brought them out from their distress; he made the storm be still, and the waves of the sea were hushed. Then they were glad because they had quiet, and he brought them to their desired haven (verses 28-30).

In the calm and storms of life, when our courage melts away, when we have a hard time finding our footing, so may we also cry out to the Lord, and may the Lord continue to guide us and bring us safely home.

As you cared for your disciples in their distress, Teacher, care for us today. For those facing literal storms of wind and water, we call on your great mercy and deliverance. Still the storms around the world. For those facing other storms of life, we call on your great love and compassion. Bring healing and wholeness. Peace, be still. Amen.

Proper 8 / Ordinary Time 13
Mark 5:21-43

Power and Particularity

As a high school student, I wrote many "compare and contrast" essays, comparing and contrasting two characters in a novel, two sides of a debate, two books on the same subject. Later as a Bible college instructor, I would ask my students to compare and contrast Paul's teaching on grace without having to work for it and James' teaching that faith without works is dead. I always found comparing and contrasting to be a useful exercise that yielded new insight.

In today's Gospel Lesson, it might be tempting to separate Mark's two stories and explore them one at a time: first the story of the young girl that Jesus raised from the dead, and then the story of the woman healed from a long illness. Each story relates a unique encounter with Jesus that can stand on its own. Yet the two stories appear together, one embedded in the other. Perhaps Mark meant simply to preserve the order of events as they happened, but the literary form of a story within a story invites us to explore them both together. As we compare and contrast them, may we also be led to fresh insight.

The first story begins when a leader of the synagogue came to Jesus for help.

Jairus' young daughter was so sick that the desperate father feared she might die. He begged Jesus to come and heal her, and Jesus went with him in spite of the great crowd gathered around.

That's when the second story interrupted the first. In the crowd that day was a woman who had been suffering from a severe illness for twelve years. She too was desperate, and she believed that if she could just touch Jesus' clothes, she would be healed. That's exactly what happened! Unnoticed by the crowd, the woman managed to get close enough to Jesus to touch his cloak, and her health was restored.

But Jesus noticed. He stopped. Looking around at the crowd, he asked, "Who touched my clothes?" The disciples were confused by his question, because so many people were pressed around them, but the woman knew that Jesus was looking for her. So she fell at his feet and told him what she had done. "Daughter," Jesus gently addressed her, "Your faith has made you well; go in peace, and be healed of your disease" (v. 34).

Then the first story continued with the arrival of people from Jairus' household. "Your daughter is dead," they reported to the leader of the synagogue. "Why trouble the teacher any further?" (v. 35). But the story of Jairus' daughter didn't end there. Instead, Jesus continued to Jairus' house. He went to the child's bedside with her parents and with the three disciples who were with him. He took the child's hand, called for her to rise, and immediately she got up!

The text tells us that Jairus' daughter was just twelve years old. The woman healed by Jesus had struggled with her illness for twelve years. Both were part of the house of Israel. Both were in need of a miracle. Both were restored immediately by the power of Jesus. Both remain unnamed in the text.

Jairus' daughter had a strong advocate in her father. As a leader of the synagogue, he was well connected, and his role meant their family held a prominent position in their community. The woman healed by Jesus was apparently alone in the crowd with no one to help her. Her terrible illness had isolated her, for it made her religiously unclean. She had no advocate. No standing in her community. She had no money since she had spent it all on doctors.

Jesus raised Jairus' daughter in the privacy of her room in her family's home. Jairus had come to Jesus in the midst of a crowd of people. While his plea for Jesus' help was personal, it was also public. But Jesus would not allow the crowd to follow him to Jairus' house. He took with him only three disciples, Peter, James, and John. And when he saw the noisy crowd of mourners already at Jairus' house, he dismissed them too. Only the girl's parents and Jesus' three disciples were witnesses to the miracle. When the girl rose from the dead at the words of Jesus, he told those who were there to get her something to eat and to tell no one about what had happened. The girl's father had come to Jesus in the midst of a crowd, but Jesus shielded her from public eye.

In contrast, Jesus publicly identified the woman in the crowd who had touched his cloak. She had come to him quietly, unnoticed by others, and perhaps she would have preferred to remain that way. Why draw attention to her disease that made her unclean? Why let everyone know about her very personal problem? But Jesus singled her out.

She had indeed been restored to physical health, and by publicly identifying her, Jesus also restored her as a full member of the community. He addressed her as "daughter." Her isolation was over!

Taken together, these two stories give witness to the breadth of Jesus' ministry. He healed a woman suffering in the midst of a long-standing disease. When a young girl succumbed to her illness and died, he raised her from the dead. One was alone, the other from a prominent family that could advocate for her. Jesus' attention and healing did not depend on their social standing or on the amount of money they had. He did not discriminate as if one were more worthy than the other. His power touched them both.

At the same time, Jesus did not ignore their particular circumstances. Given the woman's isolation, he pronounced her healing publicly and restored her to her community. It was as if her physical healing was not yet complete without the healing of her relationships. For it was only after Jesus had called her out of the crowd that he pronounced her well. Yet given the young age of Jairus' daughter, Jesus protected her privacy. She was already surrounded by too many professional mourners and other hangers-on. So he sent them away, shielded her from their skepticism, and only then called her back to life. His healing ministry was not one-size-fits-all, not a cookie-cutter ministry that treated everyone the same. Instead, he cared for each one according to their needs.

The power and particularity of Jesus' ministry is demonstrated throughout the gospels. He healed men and women, from disturbing spirits and physical ailments, at many different times and in different places, including in the synagogue on the Sabbath. He multiplied loaves and fishes to feed the crowds. He stilled wind and waves and walked on water. In Mark 5 just before our Gospel Lesson, Jesus healed a man with an unclean spirit. This man had been so distressed that he lived among the tombs, howling and hurting himself. But Jesus restored him to full health, and the man returned to his friends and his own home. This is why the crowd of people had gathered around Jesus. This is why Jairus and the woman in the crowd approached Jesus for healing. His power had become so well known among the people.

Yet although Jesus performed many wonders for many people, he treated each person according to their particular circumstances. To the man he cured at the tombs, Jesus said, "Go home to your friends, and tell them how much the Lord has done for you, and what mercy he has shown you" (Mark 5:19). To the two blind men who received their sight, he said, "See that no one knows of this" (Matthew 9:30). While he raised Jairus' daughter back to life away from the crowds, he raised a widow's son at the town gate where his body was being carried out (Luke 7:12). He sometimes healed with a word, sometimes with a touch, sometimes in public, sometimes more privately, and always with compassion.

So too for us today. Wherever we may need healing and restoration, Jesus reaches out powerfully and particularly to you and me and everyone. Our needs are different, and Jesus' power and compassion will minister to us in different ways. Yet he hears us when we call. He meets us where we are. He heals us and raises us to new life.

Life-giving Spirit, who worked powerfully in Jesus to heal and restore, have mercy on us. You see us. You see me and my particular needs and peculiarities. So heal our broken places around the world. Heal me — body, mind, soul, and spirit. Restore our broken communities, restore us to one another, and make us whole. Amen.

Proper 9 / Ordinary Time 14
Mark 6:1-13

Lessons in Perseverance and Letting Go

When I submitted my first book proposal, I was delighted to receive a positive response! The acquisitions editor had reviewed my book title, summary, outline, and sample portions, and said he would be interested in seeing my manuscript when it was finished.

So I worked on the book, completed my manuscript, sent it in, and eagerly waited for his response. I waited. And waited. And waited. And when his letter of response finally arrived — oh no! I discovered that my initial success had evaporated. On further consideration, the editor had decided not to accept my book manuscript for publication.

Rejected! The editor didn't use that word, but that's how I felt, no matter how nicely he tried to put it in his letter. While my book was well written, he wasn't sure that sales would be strong enough for the publishing house to move ahead. He was sorry, but he would have to turn down my book.

My feelings of rejection mixed with deep disappointment and confusion. Why couldn't the editor have told me this when he first read my proposal? Why did I have to spend all that time finishing my book manuscript only to have him say no? Was all that work for nothing?

When Jesus returned to his hometown, he also met with some initial success. His disciples had followed him, and when they went to the synagogue on the sabbath, Jesus began to teach. Those who were gathered that day were "astounded." How had Jesus learned to speak that way? How had he gained such wisdom? When they heard of the miraculous healings that he had performed, they marveled at his power. Here was one of their own — having gone away and done mighty things, now back home, accompanied by a band of followers, and teaching like a rabbi in the synagogue.

Yet the people's favorable response quickly turned. They knew Jesus and his family. He was a tradesman who worked with his hands, not a rabbi. He was the son of Mary. Perhaps they thought of him that way because his father, Joseph, had already died. Or perhaps they had questions about the legitimacy of Jesus' birth, so they refrained from acknowledging him according to custom as the son of Joseph. In any case, they knew Jesus' brothers and sisters, and they thought they knew him. He was one of them, not a wonder worker.

Our text says that they "took offense at him." Who did Jesus think he was? He might have brought followers with him, he might be teaching in the synagogue, but he had no rabbinical training, no official standing. Jesus might refer to himself as a prophet, but they refused to accept his claim. They didn't believe him.

As a result, our Gospel Lesson says that "he could do no deed of power there." That statement was qualified, however, since the text goes on to say that Jesus did cure some of the people who were sick. Though but a few, some did believe. Some did come to him for healing, and they certainly experienced his power. But there were no hometown crowds flocking to Jesus, no healing of the multitudes as he had done at the seaside (Mark 3:7-11). Their lack of belief kept the people from coming to Jesus and being healed.

How disappointed Jesus must have been! The Pharisees and Herodians were already conspiring against him (Mark 3:6). Scribes from Jerusalem had already accused him of having a demon (Mark 3:22). Even his family didn't understand his ministry (Mark 3:21). And now his hometown? Those who at first seemed glad to receive him soon turned away.

Perhaps Jesus had envisioned their quick rejection when he told the parable of the sower scattering seed (Mark 4:1-9). Some seed fell on rocky ground where the seed sprouted quickly, but the thin soil prevented the seed from taking root, and it withered away. So too in his hometown, whatever initial success he had among the people soon withered away.

But their rejection didn't put an end to Jesus' ministry. Instead, he went to the surrounding villages. Instead, he sent his disciples out in pairs to continue his work. Jesus called them and instructed them on their mission, on what to take with them and what to leave behind, where they should stay and how they should respond if people refused them. On Jesus' authority, they proclaimed repentance, cast out demons, anointed those who were sick, and healed them.

A close look at Jesus' instructions shows his concern for the essentials. His disciples were to wear their regular tunic and sandals, and carry a staff, but nothing more. They were to follow the regular custom of relying on whatever hospitality was offered to them, and not move from house to house in search of more convenient or comfortable or luxurious accommodations. If anyone refused to hear them, the disciples were to move on, shaking off the dust of that place behind them. This too was customary — for Jews when they left Gentile territory, and practiced also by the apostle Paul and Barnabas when they took their leave from those who would not accept their message (Acts 13:51, 18:6).

By following Jesus' instructions, the disciples could live simply and remain focused on their mission, unconcerned with material gain or popularity. They were to deal with rejection as Jesus did — by continuing with the work. Just as Jesus did not lash out at those who refused his message, so the disciples were not to take out any feelings of disappointment or confusion or anger on the people they encountered. They were simply to move on and reach out to others who might be more receptive of their mission.

When I wrote my first book, I knew it couldn't compare with Jesus' mission. It wasn't on the same level as his call and commissioning of his first disciples. But I thought of my writing as a small offering, as a way of participating in sharing the good news, as a way of sharing healing and hope with others. So I tried to deal with the rejection the way Jesus did.

I kept on with the work by sending out my book proposal to another publisher. And another. And another. Eight times I sent it out, and eight times, I received a no. Until one day, yes! My book would finally be published!

I'm grateful for that first book and that first publishing house that took a chance on me. And even more, I'm grateful for the lessons of perseverance I learned along the way. Rejection doesn't have to be the last word. Instead, it might point us in a new direction. It might help us develop a greater sense of purpose, help us refine our goals and sharpen our skills. In my case, those rejections gave me time to rewrite my manuscript and gain some maturity as a writer.

I'm grateful too for the lessons of letting ago I learned along the way. Instead of thinking so narrowly about writing for a publisher or an editor or even for a reading public, I realized that my writing was a step of faith and a service rendered to God. So whether my writing was accepted for publication or not, what really mattered was offering it up to God. And that goes for everything that you or I might do — our family life, friendships, jobs, volunteer work, leisure activities.

Whatever failures or rejections we might experience in any of these areas, instead of focusing on the rejection, may we instead set our sights on God's will and way. May we remember Jesus' instructions to his disciples: to travel lightly, so we may follow God's call in our lives.

Where have you experienced rejection, and how did you respond? How did you change direction? Did you become defensive or pushy in any way? What lessons of perseverance and letting go have you learned?

Dear Jesus, you knew the pain of rejection throughout your life and ministry, and most profoundly in your death on the cross. Yet you bore it all with good grace and trust in God. You continued the work set before you all the way to the cross. As we also face rejection and disappointments in this life, may we learn from you. May we persevere in following your example. May we let go of striving for material gain or popularity. May we place our trust in you. Amen.

Proper 10 / Ordinary Time 15
Mark 6:14-29

A Gruesome Death and God's Good News

The gospel of Mark opens with these words of hope: "The beginning of the good news of the Son of God." This is a new beginning! This is good news! This is the story of the Son of God!

Why then, does the gospel include the long, gruesome, story of the death of John the Baptist? Herod's execution of John the Baptist was no new beginning, but part of the old, familiar story in human history of power gone wrong. What happened in Herod's court was bad news. The name of Jesus appears just once at the start of our Gospel Lesson, and the Son of God is scarcely mentioned in the rest of the text.

Mark's gospel not only includes the death of John the Baptist, but it presents a more detailed account than any other gospel, fifteen verses compared to the twelve verses in the gospel of Matthew. The gospel of Luke mentions the death of John the Baptist only in a passing comment by Herod, and the gospel of John notes only his imprisonment.

Where is the good news in the death of John the Baptist? And what makes his story part of the story of the Son of God?

Throughout all four gospels, in many ways, the story of John the Baptist *is* the story of Jesus as the Son of God. Humanly speaking, they were related to one another through their mothers. John's mother, Elizabeth was a relative of Jesus' mother, Mary. Moreover, the relationship between Jesus and John went beyond human kinship.

Both were the subject of prophecy. Long before John went into the desert, the prophet Isaiah saw his role as Jesus' forerunner: "A voice cries out: 'In the wilderness prepare the way of the Lord; make straight in the desert a highway for our God'" (Isaiah 40:3). Long before the birth of Jesus, the prophet Isaiah also foretold his coming: "For a child has been born for us, a son given to us; authority rests upon his shoulders, and he is named Wonderful Counselor, Mighty God, Everlasting Father, Prince of Peace" (Isaiah 9:6).

The angel Gabriel announced the coming birth of John to his father, Zechariah, then announced the coming birth of Jesus to his mother, Mary. As an adult, Jesus affirmed John's ministry by coming to him for baptism. John respected Jesus, calling him "the Lamb of God who takes away the sin of the world" (John 1:29). John said of Jesus, "And I myself have seen and have testified that this is the Son of God." (John 1:34). While doubts would come to John when he was in prison, he faced them honestly and addressed them directly by sending two of his disciples to Jesus to ask, "Are you the one who is to come, or are we to wait for another?" (Matthew 11:3).

After Jesus reassured John by pointing to the blind receiving their sight, the deaf hearing, and other miraculous signs, Jesus went on to speak positively of John as a prophet, just as Jesus thought of himself as a prophet too. As prophets, both faced criticism and rejection — some accused John of having a demon just as they accused Jesus of having a demon. Both Jesus and John were teachers. Both had disciples. Both were eventually arrested and executed. They were so closely related that when Herod first heard about Jesus, he wondered aloud whether Jesus was John raised from the dead.

In the gospel of Mark, the death of John the Baptist foreshadows the death of Jesus. John was arrested without just cause. Yes, he had criticized Herod for marrying Herodias — while a woman might legitimately marry her husband's brother if her husband had died, Herod's brother was still very much alive, yet Herodias had left him to marry Herod. John was openly critical of the couple, which infuriated both Herod and Herodias. In fact, Herodias was so incensed that she wanted to kill John. But John had done nothing illegal. There was no legitimate reason for him to be executed or even in prison.

So too, Jesus was arrested without just cause. The religious authorities accused Jesus of blasphemy, but Pilate guessed that they were jealous of Jesus' popularity with the people. He too found no legitimate reason for Jesus to be executed or even under arrest.

Herod did not want to execute John. He had thought it enough to have John imprisoned — to protect him from Herodias and to be entertained by listening to him. Besides, Herod was afraid of John, for even he could sense that John was a holy man. But then the daughter of Herodias danced for Herod's guests, and Herod was so pleased that he made the rash promise to give her whatever she asked. He never thought that she would ask for the head of John the Baptist — on a platter! Herod felt he had no choice but to keep his word. He had been outmaneuvered and ordered John's death.

Just as Herod had not wanted to execute John the Baptist, so Pilate did not want to execute Jesus. He wanted no part of the death of an innocent man. He thought it would be enough to have Jesus flogged for causing such trouble and then released. But the crowd insisted, and Pilate felt he had no choice but to let them have their way. He too was out-maneuvered, and handed Jesus over to be crucified.

John died a gruesome death, beheaded by one of Herod's soldiers, who then delivered John's head on a platter as the daughter of Herodias had asked. Jesus died a gruesome death on the cross, suffering for hours until he finally drew his last breath. John's disciples came for his body and laid it in a tomb. Joseph of Arimathea asked for Jesus' body and laid it in a tomb.

In life and death, John the Baptist was truly Jesus' forerunner. His birth foreshadowed the coming of Jesus. His preaching prepared the way for Jesus' preaching and teaching. The circumstances around his arrest and death were later mirrored in Jesus' own arrest and execution. In many ways, the story of John the Baptist foretold Jesus' story as the Son of God, the story that Mark wanted to tell from the start of his gospel.

And what of the good news? For that, we need to look beyond the death of John the Baptist. Once again, the gospel of Mark uses a story within a story to make a point, for the death of John the Baptist does not stand alone. Instead, Mark embeds this gruesome story within another story of Jesus sending his disciples on their mission.

Just before the story of John's death, Mark 6 opens with the rejection of Jesus by the people of his hometown. Instead of lashing out at them, Jesus moved on to the surrounding villages. He continued his ministry of teaching and healing. What's more, he expanded his mission by calling, commissioning, and sending out his disciples. They too engaged in preaching, teaching, healing, and casting out demons.

The action of Mark's story is then interrupted with his long account of the death of John the Baptist. The gospel includes details of Herod's banquet, how the daughter of Herodias came in to dance, and how Herodias told her daughter to ask for the head of John the Baptist. But then immediately after the story of John's death, Mark continues the story of Jesus' disciples, how they returned from their mission and told Jesus "all that they had done and taught" (Mark 6:30).

This finally is the good news! The story of John's horrible death is not the end of the story. In spite of the rejection experienced by Jesus, in spite of John's gruesome death, in spite of Jesus' death still to come, God is still at work. When everything seems to go terribly wrong, when the end seems to be upon us, God is still at work.

Jesus tried to teach this to his disciples before his arrest and crucifixion. He told them he would be killed — but his death would not be the end of the story, for he would rise again. Yet they could not understand it. It was only after Jesus had risen from the dead, after they saw the empty tomb, after they saw him standing among them, that they could begin to grasp his teaching. God was at work in Jesus, who had risen from the dead! That was their new beginning! That finally was their good news!

God at work in Jesus Christ, be at work by your Spirit in our lives today. When bad news threatens to overwhelm us, strengthen us with your good news. Where there is pain and sorrow, bring relief and courage. Where there is suffering and death, bring new life. Amen.

Proper 11 / Ordinary Time 16
Mark 6:30-34, 53-56

Clamoring Crowd, Compassionate Shepherd

I grew up in the city, so my only encounters with sheep took place at the petting zoo or seeing them from a distance through a car window on a drive through the country. Other than that, all I know about sheep I learned from reading about them. Which is to say I don't know much about sheep at all, and I know even less about shepherds. Through the car window, I never saw a shepherd with the sheep, and the few sheep at the petting zoo didn't seem to need a shepherd.

So what does Mark 6 mean about the crowds around Jesus being "like sheep without a shepherd"? In my limited experience, sheep seem to do just fine on their own.

But that's not how it was in the ancient world of the Bible. First of all, sheep and shepherds seemed to be everywhere. In the Old Testament, Abraham and Sarah, the patriarch and matriarch of the Israelite people, were rich in livestock, with sheep, oxen, donkeys, and camels (Genesis 12:16). Before he became the king of Israel, David was a shepherd boy (1 Samuel 16:11-13). The prophet Amos was a shepherd in Tekoa, not far from Jerusalem (Amos 1:1). In the New Testament, angels appeared to shepherds in the fields and announced the birth of Jesus (Luke 2:8-20).

In biblical times, sheep were not simply part of the scenery or kept as pets to entertain children. When I was a child, that was all I knew about sheep. But in the Bible, sheep were essential to the economy and to the people's religious practice. They were valuable animals for they provided milk and meat, wool for clothing, their hides for tents. They were part of the sacrificial system as burnt offerings, sin offerings, guilt offerings, thank offerings, and offerings of well-being.

Shepherds were also essential. They watched over their sheep to protect them from wild animals. They could fend off predators with their shepherd's staff, or use stones and a sling as David had done when he watched his father's sheep. Shepherds could stand watch over their flocks at night in the open fields, or count the sheep as they entered the sheep fold. They shut the gate behind the sheep and guarded them against robbers. During the day, they led their flocks to pasture and water. They carried the weak lambs when necessary and searched for any sheep that might have fallen behind or gotten lost.

In the Old Testament tradition, sheep and shepherd also served as vivid word pictures to describe the people of Israel and the God who created and called them together. "We are the people of his pasture and the sheep of his hand," says the psalmist (Psalm 95:7). "Know that the Lord is God. It is he who made us, and we are his; we are his people and the sheep of his pasture" (Psalm 100:3).

At the start of Psalm 23, "The Lord is my shepherd; I shall not want" — because God leads me and provides for me, just like a good shepherd leads his sheep to green pastures and still waters. The prophet Isaiah offers a tender image of God as the good shepherd, who gathers the lambs in his arms and holds them close, who gently leads the mother sheep and feeds the entire flock (Isaiah 40:11).

Sheep and shepherds were also fitting metaphors for the people and their leaders. Like good shepherds, their leaders were to care for them and watch over their well-being. But so often they failed. They cared for themselves instead of caring for their people! As God said through the prophet Ezekiel, "Ah, you shepherds of Israel who have been feeding yourselves! Should not shepherds feed the sheep? You eat the fat, you clothe yourselves with the wool, you slaughter the fatlings; but you do not feed the sheep" (Ezekiel 34:2-3).

So God promised: "I myself will be the shepherd of my sheep... I will seek the lost, and I will bring back the strayed, and I will bind up the injured, and I will strengthen the weak . . . I will feed them with justice" (Ezekiel 34: 15-16). That's how a good shepherd should care for his sheep.

And that's how Jesus had compassion on the crowd that clamored for his attention. They were like sheep without a shepherd — milling around and hanging on Jesus' every word so that he and his disciples had no time even to eat. They had no space to themselves, for the crowds followed them even when they took a boat to what they thought would be a deserted place. The crowds rushed ahead to meet them there too.

Like a good shepherd, Jesus had compassion on the crowds. Instead of getting away to rest with his disciples, he spent a long day teaching and feeding the people. And the next day — after Jesus finally had time alone to pray, after the disciples got back in the boat and

Jesus walked on the water to join them, after they finally arrived at Gennesaret — again they were faced with more crowds of people like sheep without a shepherd. Wherever Jesus went, people came to him for healing, and those unable to walk were brought by others. Like the woman who found healing by touching Jesus' cloak (Mark 5:25-34), those who had heard about her experience of healing begged to touch Jesus' cloak too.

Jesus sometimes spoke of his mission to the "lost sheep" of Israel (Matthew 15:24; cf. 10:6). When the Pharisees and scribes criticized him for eating with tax collectors and others they judged as "sinners," Jesus told the parable of the lost sheep and the joy of finding it in the wilderness and carrying it home (Luke 15:1-7). He spoke of himself as the good shepherd who knows and cares for his sheep, who would lay down his life for his sheep (John 10:11-18).

Unlike the false shepherds in Israel's history who cared for themselves instead of caring for their people, Jesus cared for the people more than he cared for his own life. He gave up his life just as he said he would: "No one takes it from me, but I lay it down of my own accord. I have power to lay it down, and I have power to take it up again" (John 10:18). Truly, Jesus was and is "the great shepherd of the sheep" (Hebrews 13:20).

The sheep and shepherd motif is a powerful one even for someone like me with little direct experience with sheep or shepherds. In some ways, I am one of the sheep, created by God and dependent on his care and leading. I'm grateful for Jesus as the great shepherd who gave his life to save me, who has compassion on me, who finds me when I lose my way, who heals and restores me, who rejoices over me, and carries me home.

Yet in other ways, I am a kind of shepherd too, responsible to care for others, to exercise compassion, to strengthen the weak, to be generous with my time and energy as Jesus was. Am I feeding others, or only myself? Do I put myself first at the expense of others? Ezekiel's words of prophecy against the false shepherds of Israel stand in contrast to the example of Jesus, and challenge all of us today.

We may not have crowds clamoring after us as Jesus did. But we all have roles and responsibilities at home and work, in our churches and community. Whatever our particular calling or station in life, we need to use our positions and powers wisely — not to abuse the weak, but to respect and encourage them; not to enlarge our own reputation, but to build others up; not to destroy, but to heal and restore.

Like sheep, may we know our good shepherd and follow him. May we rest in his care and know we are loved. Like good shepherds, may we be generous in compassion and in serving others. May we be faithful and practice justice and mercy for the good of all.

Jesus, Good Shepherd, guide and guard us in all things. Strengthen us to serve the people you place in our care and to carry out the tasks you set before us. When we follow you by quiet waters, lift our hearts in gratitude for your goodness. When the valley deepens, grant us courage and comfort still to follow you. For we are the sheep of your pasture. Amen.

Proper 12 / Ordinary Time 17
John 6:1-21

God of the Possible and Impossible

On a world scale and in our personal lives, we face all kinds of apparently impossible situations. Situations that are difficult and stressful, and that seem beyond our abilities to solve. Armed conflicts in Ukraine, Afghanistan, and elsewhere around the world. Famine and critical food insecurity in South Sudan, Somalia, Yemen, and other countries. Ongoing racism, sexual abuse, and other social ills in our own country. That stack of bills at home that just keeps growing. Worry over one of the children. Worry over a frail parent. Frustration at work or the fear of losing the job altogether. Waiting for test results from the doctor's office. A Monday morning math exam. A falling out with a friend that you don't know how to fix.

In our Gospel Lesson today, Jesus and his disciples faced an apparently impossible situation too: a crowd of hungry people and no food. Our text says the crowd numbered "about five thousand in all" (v. 10). All hungry. All needing to be fed. On the far shore of the Sea of Galilee, up on the mountain. With no McDonald's, no Kroger's, no other place for takeout or groceries.

So Jesus turned to one of his disciples named Philip and asked, "Where are we to buy bread for these people to eat?" It was an odd question up on the mountain. For even if there were a place to buy bread, Jesus and his disciples certainly didn't have the money to feed such a large crowd. It just wasn't possible for them to buy enough bread for everyone.

So Philip replied, "Six months' wages would not buy enough bread for each of them to get a little." The amount was 200 denarii — what a day laborer might earn in about six months of work. That was a lot of money that the disciples didn't have. Their financial resources were hopelessly inadequate for such a large crowd. And the food supply in that area couldn't feed that many people anyway. To Philip's practical way of thinking, this was an apparently impossible situation.

Now there's nothing wrong with being practical. In fact, we need to be practical. In the face of natural disaster, it's important to assess the damage — to find out who and how many are affected, to identify the immediate needs. When we're under financial stress, then we need to be even more practical than usual about where we spend our money, and where we make do. We need to ask practical questions when we're approached for money. If we've got an impossible math exam coming up, we need to ask practical questions about when the exam will be and what will be covered. But sometimes being practical is not enough. When he took a practical look at the hungry crowd, Philip knew there was simply no way to feed them.

At the same time, one of Jesus' other disciples seemed to be taking stock of the crowd. Andrew was a fisherman, a businessman used to working with others as part of a crew, used to working with others in business. So he quite naturally looked around the crowd for others to partner with, for people who might be able to help. He said to Jesus, "There is a boy here who has five barley loaves and two fish,"

Barley was the food of the poor, and barley loaves were generally small, perhaps the size of an English muffin. In the original Greek, the two small fish were actually two small pieces of fish, most likely pickled fish, which was common in that area of Galilee. In other words, this boy was carrying a poor boy's lunch — just a few sardine sandwiches. That was all he had, but he was ready and willing to give it. He was ready and willing to do what he could.

As we face apparently impossible situations today, we can also be ready and willing to do what we can. We can face that impossible health challenge by doing what we can to take care of ourselves with healthy food, exercise, getting enough sleep, and consulting with health professionals. We can study for that impossible exam. We can pray for peace. We can give to famine relief.

And we don't need to do these things alone. Like Andrew, who looked to the crowd and saw the young boy with his lunch, we can look around to see who else might be willing to help. If you're facing an impossible situation today, if you're feeling overwhelmed by your job, your family, your finances, if you have health concerns, whatever you face — you can look around for help. For people who will pray, who can offer wise counsel and personal encouragement, who have business and financial expertise, who have a wealth of knowledge about community resources, who have experience in many different areas.

We can be practical like Philip and look around for help like Andrew. We can do our part like the boy with his lunch. But all our human effort can only take us so far. Our impossible health situation may still be impossible even when we do all we can to eat healthy food and get enough exercise and rest. Even if we give all we can, our donations are still so small in the face of great need. As Andrew said about the boy's few sardine sandwiches, "What are they among so many people?"

But Jesus already knew what he would do. "Make the people sit down," he said. So everyone sat down on the grass. Then Jesus took the small barley loaves, gave thanks, and distributed the bread. He took the two small pieces of fish, gave thanks for them, and passed them around. He gave the people as much as they wanted, and when everyone had eaten, he said to his disciples, "Gather up the fragments that are left over, so that nothing may be lost." The disciples collected twelve baskets of leftovers!

When appealing for funds, organizations like the Red Cross sometimes arrange for donations to be matched one-to-one. So if you give a hundred dollars, your donation will be multiplied so the organization receives two hundred dollars. That's one way of multiplying what people give. But Jesus did much better than that. In the hands of Jesus, the five small loaves and the two pieces of fish became enough to feed an entire crowd with plenty of leftovers. The boy's small lunch wasn't matched one to one or even a hundred to one. Instead, Jesus multiplied the boy's lunch to feed a crowd of five thousand. And Jesus didn't feed the people a modest snack to tide them over until they could get home for some real food. He fed them until they had enough, with twelve baskets of bread to spare. In the face of overwhelming need, Jesus did more than enough.

Our text calls this miracle a "sign" because it showed the people something about Jesus. "This is indeed the prophet," they said. And in our Gospel Lesson, this sign is immediately followed by another. That evening, the disciples got into a boat to cross the sea back to Capernaum. Jesus remained on shore for some time alone, and later walked out to the boat which was a few miles off shore. Jesus walked on the sea! The disciples were terrified, but this too was a sign.

Taken together, these two stories of Jesus feeding the crowd and walking on the sea are signs pointing to Jesus as God. They tell us that no matter what our situation — God is great. God provides for us. God is present with us.

Whatever our impossible situation, whatever our difficulty or challenge — we need a bit of Philip to be practical and realistic; we need a bit of the boy and his lunch to give what we can toward a solution; we need a bit of Andrew to call on others for help; but most of all, we need God who acts beyond our practical expectations, who comes to us where we are; who can take what little we have and multiply our resources and our efforts, who can help us work together and support one another, who redefines what is possible.

God of the possible and impossible, we rely on your faithful presence and provision for all our needs. When we face what looks impossible, remind us that all things are possible with you. You make a new way in the wilderness. You multiply meager resources to be more than enough. Transform our fear into faith, that we might trust in you. Amen.

Proper 13 / Ordinary Time 18
John 6:24-35

Food That Perishes, Food That Endures

Rapid fire "this or that" questions can make good ice breakers or be a fun game between friends. So, tea or coffee? Glass half full or glass half empty? Crunchy peanut butter or smooth? Camping or glamping?

A talk show host might use a series of such questions as a quick introduction to the next guest. But when it comes time for the more in-depth interview, the questions tend to get longer and more thoughtful.

When the crowds finally caught up with Jesus on the other side of the sea, they asked him three pointed questions. They already knew his reputation as a preacher and healer. They had already heard his teaching for themselves the day before. They had already received the bread and fish that he had multiplied to feed them. They didn't need an ice breaker this or that question. They were ready for an in-depth question-and-answer session. But with each question they asked, Jesus urged them to go deeper still.

The crowd began with what seemed like a straightforward inquiry: "Rabbi, when did you come here?" (verse 25).

After the miraculous meal the night before, the people had seen Jesus' disciples leave without him and in the only boat. The next morning, they saw no boat, no disciples, and no Jesus. So when other boats arrived from Tiberias, some of the crowd went on board and sailed with them to Capernaum to look for Jesus (John 6:22-24). When they found him, it was only natural for them to wonder when Jesus arrived and how he managed to get there.

But instead of answering their question, Jesus directed them to another, deeper, issue. Why were they looking for him at all? The night before, some in the crowd had wanted to make him king. Why not crown a king who could feed a great crowd with just a few loaves of bread and pieces of fish? Why not crown a king who could provide enough for everyone? At the time, Jesus simply withdrew from them. Now he pointed out that they had been drawn only by the plentiful food. That was why they were looking for him — and that was precisely the problem. Instead of looking only for physical food, Jesus re-directed them to think of "the food that endures for eternal life."

Jesus clearly cared about the people's physical needs, and the people knew that. They had eaten the bread and fish. They had heard of his miraculous healings. Jesus had even healed the son of a royal official (John 4:46-54). He had even healed a man on the Sabbath (John 5:1-15). When Jesus taught his disciples to pray, he included "Give us this day our daily bread" (Matthew 6:11).

At the same time, Jesus' compassion for the people went beyond their physical needs, beyond "the food that perishes" to "the food that endures for eternal life." When he healed the son of the royal official, the son recovered physically, *and* the whole household came to believe in Jesus. When he healed the man on the Sabbath, the man's ability to walk was restored, *and* he went on to share his story. In the Lord's prayer, along with praying for daily bread, Jesus also included prayer for God's kingdom and will, for forgiveness from sin, for protection in times of trial.

Instead of focusing only on their physical needs, Jesus challenged the crowd to think more broadly about their spiritual needs as well, to go beyond their earthly concerns to the things of heaven.

Their second question managed to go a little deeper: "What must we do to perform the works of God?" (verse 28).

Perhaps they were thinking of the ten commandments. Or of the many other laws that were part of Jewish religious life. Did they really need to keep all of them? The Old Testament prophet Micah had offered this summary: "What does the Lord require of you, but to do justice and to love kindness and to walk humbly with your God" (Micah 6:8). What would Jesus say?

Jesus replied, "This is the work of God, that you believe in him whom he has sent" (verse 29).

In the other gospel accounts, and in some of the New Testament letters, "believe" appears in noun form as belief or faith. So Romans 3:28 speaks of being justified by faith. Galatians 5:22 lists faith as part of the fruit of the Spirit. But in the gospel of John, believe is always a verb, an action word. So Jesus said to the Samaritan woman at the well, "Believe me" (John 4:21). Simon Peter said, "We have come to believe and know that you are the Holy One of God" (John 6:29). The blind man who received his sight said, "Lord, I believe" (John 9:38).

Believing is not only an action word. It is relational. So Jesus said to the woman at the well, "Believe *me*." He said to his disciples, "Do not let your hearts be troubled. Believe in God; believe also in *me*" (John

14:1). This is no abstract belief. It's not a set of principles. In John's gospel, believing is about relationship, so it might be translated as "trust" or "entrusting."

The work of God is this: to trust in Jesus.

That didn't mean Jesus was anti-law or anti-work. Jesus kept the law. He honoured God above all. He did not take God's name in vain. He kept the Sabbath in life-giving ways. He did not steal or murder. He did not covet. Jesus worked diligently. He worked as a tradesman and later in his public ministry as a teacher, preacher, and healer. He said, "My Father is still working, and I also am working" (John 5:17).

When a rich, young man asked what he should do to gain eternal life, Jesus first pointed him to the law. It was only after the man insisted that he had kept all of the law, that Jesus told him to sell all he had, give the money to the poor, and follow him (Matthew 19:16-22). Instead of narrowly focusing on the law, Jesus urged that young man to go beyond the letter of the law to place his trust in Jesus.

In speaking with the crowds, Jesus urged the people to consider their relationship with God — the one who had both given the law and sent Jesus. Whatever other laws the people might keep, whatever other work they might do, trusting in Jesus was the work that encompassed everything.

So too for us today, whatever other work we might do in this life, however long our to-do lists, this is our most basic work, the basic calling for all of us: to trust in Jesus and to live that out in all we do.

Finally, the people get to their third question: "What sign are you going to give us then, so that we may see it and believe you? What work are you performing? (verse 30).

After all that Jesus had already said and done, how could they ask such a question? Jesus' first sign had been turning water into wine for a wedding in Cana (John 2:1-11). His healing of the royal official's son had been his second sign (John 4:46-54). His third sign was miraculously providing them with loaves and fish to eat (John 6:1-14). Each of these signs was more public than the last, and each "revealed his glory" (John 2:22).

Why did Jesus need to keep on proving himself to them? The crowd needed only to look at the signs they had already been given. They needed to look beyond the bread that they had received, to see Jesus as the Bread of Life, the only bread that could truly satisfy. "I am the bread of life," Jesus said to them plainly. "Whoever believes in me will never be hungry, and whoever believes in me will never be thirsty" (verse 35). The ordinary bread that they had eaten was not so ordinary after all. Spiritually speaking, that bread was an extraordinary sign that pointed to Jesus as the bread of life.

Like the people with their three questions, I wonder if some of our questions today might also be just as shallow and misguided. Perhaps instead of turning too quickly to question God, we might consider asking these questions of ourselves: Like the crowds who questioned Jesus, are we more interested in what God can do for us than in who God is? Are we still trying to work our way to heaven instead of trusting and following Jesus? Are we still looking for a sign when the signs of God at work are all around us?

May Jesus, the Bread of Life, guide our reflection and lead us to abundant and fruitful living.

Dear Jesus, Bread of Life, we sometimes hunger after answers to the wrong questions. We sometimes hunger after miracles, and ignore the miracle of trusting in you. Teach us to ask better questions. Teach us to go deeper in our relationship with you. Feed us with the food that endures. Amen.

Proper 14 / Ordinary Time 19
John 6:35, 41-51

Bread of Earth, Bread of Heaven

"I am the bread of life. Whoever comes to me will never be hungry, and whoever believes in me will never be thirsty." If this verse sounds like a repeat from last Sunday, you're right. Jesus' declaration appears twice in the *Revised Common Lectionary* — as the climax of last week's reading and the start of this week's. The repetition underscores the importance of Jesus' words. It's a way of telling us to sit up and take notice. Don't hurry over these words. Don't pass quickly over them on the way to the rest of the gospel story. Pay attention.

But what makes these words so key? All of Jesus' teaching warrants our full attention, from what he says about signs in the gospel of John, to his parables in the gospel of Mark, his beatitudes, the Lord's prayer, his summary of the law to love God and neighbor, and so much more. With all the richness of Jesus' teaching, why are these words about the bread of life so deserving of repetition?

First of all, the repetition from last week reminds us that this Gospel Lesson continues the people's dialogue with Jesus. They have already raised three questions with him: When did you come here? What must we do? What sign will you give us? As Jesus answered each question, he re-directed them to another, deeper, issue. Instead of asking, when did you come here, they needed to examine why they were looking for Jesus in the first place. Instead of focusing on doing the works of God, they needed to recognize God at work and trust in Jesus. Instead of asking for another sign, they needed to recognize the signs they had already been given, in Jesus' feeding the five thousand in the wilderness and in his miraculous healings.

In today's Gospel Lesson, more questions surface: "Is this not Jesus, the son of Joseph, whose father and mother we know? How can he now say, 'I have come down from heaven'?" (verse 42). As part of their continuing dialogue, Jesus again re-directs the people to another, deeper, issue. Instead of being offended by his words and complaining, the people needed to learn from their own prophets and be taught by God. If they would only listen to God and learn, they would be drawn to Jesus as the one sent by God.

In this way, Jesus continues the conversation, responding to each question by re-directing the people to look more deeply at their own motives and behavior. He also continues with the metaphor of the bread — this is a second reason for the repetition of his assertion, "I am the bread of life." The people looked for Jesus because he had given them bread to eat, but they needed to look beyond the loaves of barley to see Jesus as the bread of life. They needed to look beyond the manna their ancestors ate in the wilderness. They needed to look beyond Moses. For it was God who provided their ancestors with manna — not Moses. And it was God who sent Jesus as the living bread.

The five thousand people who ate the bread in the wilderness would be hungry again. The people's ancestors who ate the manna in the wilderness were sustained for a time, but then they died. In contrast, those who receive Jesus as the living bread will never be hungry again, and they will live forever, for Jesus will raise them. In fact, those who believe have eternal life even now. Just as bread was a staple of the people's diet to sustain their physical bodies, Jesus as the living bread was essential to their spiritual life.

A third reason for the repetition of this key verse is found in the first two words, "I am." To us, this might sound like a simple declaration. But given the background and history of the people, those two words would have given them a jolt, for "I am" was the divine name that God revealed to Moses.

One day when Moses was out in the field with his father-in-law's sheep, Moses saw a bush that was burning yet not consumed by the fire. When he went to take a closer look, God called to him out of the burning bush: "I have observed the misery of my people who are in Egypt; I have heard their cry on account of their taskmasters" (Exodus 3:7). In response to the people's suffering, God chose to deliver them and bring them to a new land. God chose Moses to lead them: "Now go, I am sending you to Pharaoh to bring my people, the Israelites, out of Egypt" (Exodus 3:10).

But Moses was afraid. Who was he to lead the people out of Egypt? Who was he to lead the people anywhere? If the people were to question him, what would he say? God replied, "I am who I am... Thus you shall say to the Israelites, 'I am has sent me to you.'" (Exodus

3:14). "I am" was God's name, revealed to Moses at a critical point in the people's history.

By saying "I am," Jesus recalled Moses' encounter with God, and claimed the divine name for himself. He revealed himself as God — the one from the beginning of time, through whom all things were created, the one who could walk on water, the one who could multiply a few loaves and fish to feed five thousand people. The crowd had been quite happy to eat their fill. But once Jesus said, "I am," the people started to complain. Who did Jesus think he was? The people knew him and knew his family — or at least they thought they did.

This was not the only time that Jesus used the divine name "I am" in the gospel of John. He said it once before to the woman at the well, "I am he, the one who is speaking to you" (4:26). Then in our Gospel Lesson he says, "I am the bread of life" (verse 35) and "I am the living bread (verse 51). He would later say, "I am the light of the world" (8:12, 9:5), "before Abraham was, I am" (8:58), "I am the door of the sheep" (10:7), "I am the door" (10:9). "I am the good shepherd" (10:11), "I am the resurrection and the life" (22:36), "I am the way the truth, and the life" (14:6), "I am the true vine" (15:1). Over and over, Jesus would say "I am," often pairing it with an ordinary object from daily life and infusing it with new meaning.

So when Jesus said, "I am the bread of life," that was only one "I am" saying among many. What's more, Jesus repeated the expression several times in our reading: "I am the bread that came down from heaven" (verse 41), "I am the bread of life" (verse 48), "I am the living bread" (verse 51). What an extraordinary claim: Jesus came down from heaven, the living bread — God in the flesh, given for the life of the world!

In the crowd around Jesus that day, all were challenged to look beyond the bread of earth that they had eaten to the bread of heaven in the person of Jesus. Some were offended by his words. Some complained. Some questioned.

How do you and I respond today? Looking back from our vantage point — after the life, death, resurrection, and ascension of Jesus, after the long history of the Christian church — do we find it easier to accept Jesus' extraordinary claim? Do we accept the challenge to seek the living bread? Are we offended when God turns out to be different than we expect? Do we complain and question?

Whatever our response, may this thought continue to nourish us: God in Jesus Christ gave his life for the world — by being born in human flesh; by his ministry of preaching, teaching, and healing; by submitting to arrest, torture, and death on the cross; and rising again to new life. May God continue to draw us to Jesus as the living bread.

Bread of Heaven, nourish and sustain our life in you. When we grow hungry, feed us. When we complain, restore to us the joy of your presence. In our weakness, grant us your mercy. In our questions and confusion, grant us clarity. We look to you in faith and hope, for spiritual understanding, and strength beyond what we can see. Amen.

Proper 15 / Ordinary Time 20
John 6:51-58

Eating and Drinking by Faith

"Eat my flesh and drink my blood" (John 6:54). Read out of context, these words seem more fitting for a horror film than anything else. They seem to describe some sort of cannibalism, with the victim's active encouragement. I find the words so repulsive that I hardly want to read more, and I'm not sure that reading more is much help: "Those who eat my flesh and drink my blood have eternal life" (verse 54). Taken literally, this still sounds like a deadly exchange, with an impossible promise, made by someone who is deeply disturbed.

People would later say that Jesus was out of his mind (John 10:20), and his words about eating his flesh and drinking his blood would only have reinforced that impression. At this point, however, the Jewish leaders seemed confused. They knew the many laws that governed eating and drinking. Animals considered "unclean" were not to be eaten. The law said, "No person among you shall eat blood, nor shall any alien who resides among you eat blood" (Leviticus 17:12). So how could Jesus say, "Drink my blood?" They debated among themselves: "How can this man give us his flesh to eat?" (verse 52).

But read in the larger context of his teaching, what Jesus said about eating and drinking is clearly not to be taken literally. The flesh and the blood are not to be taken literally as human flesh and blood. At the start of our Gospel Lesson, Jesus said, "I am the living bread that came down from heaven" (verse 51) — not literally bread made with flour, water, and yeast kneaded together and baked. Instead Jesus used bread as a metaphor, as a word picture to express his life-giving presence and power. Just as physical bread nourished the physical body, so the living bread from heaven nourished the human soul and spirit.

In a similar way, Jesus used eating his flesh and drinking his blood as metaphors. Like bread, eating and drinking were part of ordinary, everyday life. But as metaphors, as word pictures, they became much more. Eating and drinking expressed the intimacy between Jesus and those who believed in him. His followers were to receive him and participate in his life so completely that his life would become their life.

This promise made to Jesus' first disciples is for us today as well. Just as food and water become part of our physical bodies, so trusting in Jesus means that Jesus becomes part of us, lives in us. "It is no longer I who live," wrote the apostle Paul, "but it is Christ who lives in me" (Galatians 2:20). That's what it means to eat the true food and drink the true drink (verse 55). By faith we receive Jesus into our lives, we become united with him, sharing in both his sufferings and the power of his resurrection (Philippians 3:10).

For the Apostle Paul, sharing in the sufferings of Jesus meant being beaten, pelted with stones, facing danger as he travelled to share the gospel, often going hungry and without sleep (2 Corinthians 11:25-28). Yet he also shared in the life of Jesus that sustained and empowered him, for he was "afflicted in every way, but not crushed; perplexed, but not driven to despair; persecuted, but not forsaken; struck down, but not destroyed" (2 Corinthians 4:7-10).

For us too, sharing in the life of Christ means sharing both his suffering and the power of his resurrection. What might that look like for us today? When we work hard at building relationships in the name of Christ only to find people turn away, when we spend long hours organizing a community event with only a lukewarm response, is that part of the suffering of Christ? And what of the power of his resurrection? When life is hard, and I grieve a terrible loss, can I draw on the strength of Christ living in me? When you feel stressed by one interruption after another and another and another, can you respond with the compassion of Christ living in you? As we face the challenges of daily life, can we become more like Jesus in loving God and loving our neighbor as we love ourselves? These are just a few examples of what it might mean for us to eat his flesh and drink his blood — not literally, but by placing our trust in Jesus and walking with him in daily life.

Unlike the other gospel accounts, the gospel of John does not include the institution of the Lord's Supper. While John describes Jesus washing his disciples' feet (John 13:1-16), there is no report of Jesus' last supper with his disciples before his arrest. No blessing of the bread and cup. No passing them around to his disciples. No sharing one last time at the table before Jesus' death.

Some scholars suggest that our Gospel Lesson today is John's version of the institution of the last supper. Our text includes the bread. It speaks of eating and drinking. It refers to Jesus' sacrifice for the life of the world. It speaks of resurrection, the promise of eternal life, and Jesus' abiding presence. Although Jesus did not give any specific words of institution in our text, it connects well with the Lord's Supper in the other gospels and with our celebration of communion today.

As we eat the bread and drink of the cup, it's not only a religious ritual. It's a way of expressing, yes, we receive Jesus into our lives. Yes, we trust him. Yes, we are one with him. Yes, his life is now our life. It doesn't mean that we're now perfect, that we'll never again fail God, fail others, or fail ourselves. It doesn't mean that we have all our questions answered, or that we have finally figured out our lives. We eat and drink not because we're perfect, but as a sign of our participation in the life of Christ.

We eat and drink together, because we are not alone in this journey. Jesus gave his life for the life of the world — not only for me, not only for you, but for all of us. Jesus is the living bread. In our text, he says twice, "whoever eats" (verse 51), "whoever eats" (verse 58). We don't choose the "whoever" in our lives, the "whoever" at this table. God draws those who come and joins us together in the body of Christ.

And God will send us out. This bit of bread and this bit of drink make a small meal — so small that it's hardly a snack, let alone a meal. But it represents God's nourishment beyond our imagination. God strengthens us for the journey beyond these walls. God energizes us for service, to be like Jesus — to act in life-giving ways even in the midst of suffering, to have compassion, to care for others, to bring his healing presence everywhere we go. Forgiven, we can forgive others. With the hope of eternal life, we can live with confidence in God.

This time of communion is not only about this time, about these moments. It's about the life we will live for the rest of today and for tomorrow. It's about our ongoing relationship with Jesus as the living bread, about him living in us.

This is reflected in the classic hymn:

> Break thou the bread of life, dear Lord, to me,
> as thou didst break the loaves beside the sea.
> Beyond the sacred page I seek thee, Lord;
> my spirit pants for thee, O Living Word!

"Break Thou the Bread of Life" has often been sung as a communion hymn, but the lyrics weren't specifically written for communion.

Instead, writer Mary Lathbury wrote these words for a summer assembly of Sunday school teachers. She wanted to encourage them to go deeper in their study and deeper in their relationship with Jesus. So she drew on Jesus' feeding of the crowds and on his self-identification as the Bread of life.

But her concern was not mainly about the celebration of the Lord's Supper. It was about seeking God in study, in the Bible, in prayer, in all of life. It was about Jesus feeding the crowds long ago and feeding us today. Jesus is the Bread of Life, our dear Lord, and living word — in times of communion and at all times.

So take and eat. Take and drink. We share in the suffering and death of Jesus. We share in his life. We are joined to Christ and joined with one another. May we abide in Christ now and forever.

O Living Word, make us hungry for you, make us thirsty for you. In faith, may we seek after you and find you. Amen.

Proper 16 / Ordinary Time 21
John 6:56-69

Turning Away or Moving Forward

When I was in university, I found myself at the first major crossroads of my adult life. I had taken two years of general studies, discovered a love for political science, and started the poli sci honors program. I didn't have a specific vocational goal, but I was curious to learn more, confident that doors would open for me as I continued my studies, and I wanted to finish my bachelor degree with honors after my name.

But the honors program proved harder than I expected. There was a lot more reading than I was used to. I felt intimidated both by the material and by my fellow students who seemed so accomplished. The professor of my honors seminar acted as if his course was the only one that mattered. And in addition to our scheduled seminars, there were extra sessions to attend.

A few weeks into the semester, I wasn't sure that I wanted to continue, and by mid-semester, I was sure. But would I really quit the path that I had started? Would I let myself be defeated by the stress, or would I power through? That was my crossroads — to continue with the program, or to turn away? I needed to decide.

That was the first major crossroads in my adult life, and there have been many more since then. We all face crossroads, important decisions with life-changing consequences. Do we continue with a relationship that's getting serious, or bring it gently to an end? Do we accept one job offer or another? Will we have children, and how many? Will we get a second opinion on a medical diagnosis? Seek alternative treatment? Will we change churches? Will we move to another part of the country or another part of the world? How will we care for aging parents? There are many roads — and many crossroads — in the journey of life.

Those who followed Jesus found themselves at a crossroads too. Some had been part of the five thousand that Jesus had miraculously fed beside the sea. Some had been physically healed of their disease or knew someone who had been. Some had heard Jesus' strange teaching about the bread of life and the bread of heaven, about eating and drinking by faith.

Some found Jesus' teaching too difficult. Perhaps some were turned off by his references to eating his flesh and drinking his blood. Perhaps they didn't understand his metaphorical language. Or maybe they understood it too well. Perhaps it was the total commitment represented by eating and drinking that seemed too hard — the commitment to share in both the suffering and the life of Jesus. So they complained and continued to question: who could accept this difficult path?

In response, Jesus had a question of his own for them: "Does this offend you?" (verse 61). If they were offended by his teaching, what if they were to see him ascending to heaven? Would that add to the offense? Or would that be enough to convince them to believe? One day they would indeed see the start of his ascent in his public execution — with his body lifted up on a cross and on display.

The Apostle Paul wrote of Christ crucified as "a stumbling block to Jews and foolishness to Gentiles" (1 Corinthians 1:23). He wrote of "the offense of the cross" (Galatians 5:11). In our Gospel Lesson, many had gone to great lengths on foot and by boat to follow Jesus. Would they now stumble and take offense? This was their crossroads: to continue following him or to turn away.

Many turned away. They stopped following Jesus and went back home, back to whatever they had been doing before they started following him. They had counted the cost and decided it was too high. How disappointing for Jesus — and yet he had known all along that some would not continue with him. He knew that some were more interested in the bread that they had eaten, than in the living bread he offered them.

For the twelve who remained, Jesus had another question: "Do you also wish to go away?" (verse 67). Jesus already knew who would betray him, so perhaps he asked the question more for the sake of his disciples than for his own. They too were at a crossroads. Would they too stumble and take offense? What would they decide? Jesus' question gave them the opportunity to consider the cost of discipleship and their own commitment. Apart from the mass crowd of would-be followers and hangers-on, apart from the leaders in the synagogue, this question was for Jesus' closest disciples.

Among the twelve, Simon Peter took it upon himself to answer for them all. He quickly responded, "Lord, to whom can we go? You have the words of eternal life. We have come to believe and know that you are the Holy One of God" (verse 69).

We might think that Peter spoke too quickly and carelessly. Unlike Jesus, he did not know who would betray him. Peter didn't know that he himself would deny even knowing Jesus. Peter would speak out too quickly at other times too. When the disciples were on the boat and saw Jesus walking on the water toward them, it was Peter who dared to say, "Lord, if it is you, command me to come to you on the water" (Matthew 14:28). When Jesus took Peter, James, and John up a mountain by themselves, it was Peter who blurted out, "Rabbi, it is good for us to be here; let us make three dwellings, one for you, one for Moses, and one for Elijah" (Mark 9:5). Peter would speak out, even when he wasn't sure what to say.

But in our gospel text, at that moment — at that particular crossroads — Peter felt sure of himself and of the others. They had come to believe — and know! — Jesus as the Holy One of God, their teacher and Lord, Bread of Life and Bread of Heaven. Peter had grown into this commitment over time. He had traveled with Jesus and seen him in action. He had heard Jesus' words of spirit and life. He must have had many conversations with Jesus and the other disciples that were never recorded — informal conversations as they walked the road together, as they gathered up the leftovers after Jesus had fed the five thousand, after seeing Jesus heal the crowds and even raise a young girl who had died. For Peter the choice at the crossroads was obvious — to whom could they go? There was no one else, but Jesus.

When I reached the crossroads in my university education, the choice gradually became obvious to me too. It took some time to admit that even to myself, but after living through the first few weeks of the semester, I had come to believe that the poli sci honors program was just not for me. I prayed about it. I talked with my parents and close friends. I consulted with a faculty adviser. Over time, I knew what I had to do. Trying to struggle through just so I could graduate with honors was foolish. I could withdraw from the program and still get my bachelors degree. And that's exactly what I did.

What crossroads are you facing in life? How have you grown into the decision that now faces you? Do you have some lived experience like Peter had with Jesus? Can you talk with other people you trust as he might have talked with his fellow disciples? Have you taken time to pray over and ponder your situation?

Are you facing a crossroads in your faith? In our age of deconstruction, many question the beliefs they grew up with and are searching for answers. Many hope to rebuild something new, while others simply turn away. When Jesus asked his disciples, "Do you also wish to go away?" the wording in the Greek text implied that Jesus expected his disciples to say no. That's how Peter responded, but what of us? How has our life experience with Jesus prepared us for the crossroads we face in matters of faith? Who do we talk to? How do we pray and ponder?

Whatever crossroads we face in life, Jesus is with us. May his teaching and example help us to choose wisely. May the power of his resurrection sustain and enable us to move forward.

Jesus, the Holy One of God, abide with us, and teach us to abide in you. When the way seems too difficult, strengthen us still to follow. Grant us your courage, wisdom, and peace. Amen.

About the Author

April Yamasaki is an ordained minister with over 25 years of experience in pastoral ministry, currently serving as resident author with Valley CrossWay Church, a liturgical worship community in Abbotsford, British Columbia, Canada. She is also editor for the devotional magazine *Rejoice!*, writes on spiritual growth and Christian living both online and in print, and speaks widely in churches and other ministry settings. This is her fourth collection of sermons for CSS Publishing. Her other books include *Sacred Pauses: Spiritual Practices for Personal Renewal* and *Four Gifts: Seeking Self-Care for Heart, Soul, Mind, and Strength*. For more information, please visit her websites, AprilYamasaki.com and WhenYouWorkfortheChurch.com.

www.ingramcontent.com/pod-product-compliance
Lightning Source LLC
Chambersburg PA
CBHW051716040426
42446CB00008B/912